# HOW TO DRAW
# ACTION
# FIGHTING
# FIGURES

## Mark Bergin

**PowerKiDS**
press

New York

Published in 2012 by The Rosen Publishing Group, Inc.
29 East 21st Street, New York, NY 10010

*Editor:* Rob Walker
*U.S. Editor:* Kara Murray

Library of Congress Cataloging-in-Publication Data

Bergin, Mark.
 Action fighting figures / by Mark Bergin. — 1st ed.
    p. cm. — (How to draw)
 ISBN 978-1-4488-6464-5 (library binding) —
 ISBN 978-1-4488-6475-1 (pbk.) —
 ISBN 978-1-4488-6476-8 (6-pack)
 1. Figure drawing—Technique—Juvenile literature.
 2. Combat in art—Juvenile literature.  I. Title.
 NC765.B38 2012
 743.4—dc22

2011017637

Manufactured in China

CPSIA Compliance Information: Batch #SW2102PK:
For Further Information contact Rosen Publishing,
New York, New York at 1-800-237-9932

PAPER FROM
SUSTAINABLE
**FORESTS**

# Contents

# Making a Start

Learning to draw is about looking and seeing. Keep practicing and get to know your subject. Use a sketchbook to make quick drawings. Start by doodling, and experiment with shapes and patterns. There are many ways to draw. This book shows only some methods. Visit art galleries, look at artists' drawings, see how friends draw, but above all, find your own way.

5

# Drawing Materials

Silhouette

ry using different types of drawing paper and materials. Experiment with charcoal, wax crayons, and pastels. All pens, from felt-tips to ballpoints, will make interesting marks. You could also try drawing with pen and ink on wet paper.

**Silhouette** is a style of drawing that mainly uses solid black shapes.

Felt-tip

**Felt-tips** come in a range of line widths. The wider pens are good for filling in large areas of flat tone.

Hard **pencils** are grayer and soft pencils are blacker. Hard pencils are graded from #4 (the hardest) through #3 to #2 1/2. A #1 pencil is a soft pencil.

Pencil

Lines drawn in **ink** cannot be erased, so keep your ink drawings sketchy and less rigid. Don't worry about mistakes as these lines can be lost in the drawing as it develops.

Ink

7

# Perspective

If you look at any object from different viewpoints, you will see that the part that is closest to you looks larger and the part farthest away from you looks smaller. Drawing in perspective is a way of creating a feeling of depth, or of showing three dimensions on a flat surface.

V.P.

The vanishing point (V.P.) is the place in a perspective drawing where parallel lines appear to meet. The position of the vanishing point depends on the viewer's eye level. Sometimes a low viewpoint can give your drawing added drama.

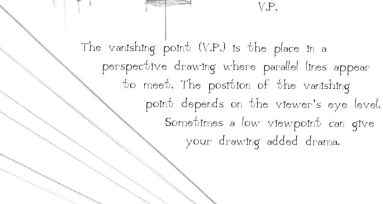

V.P.

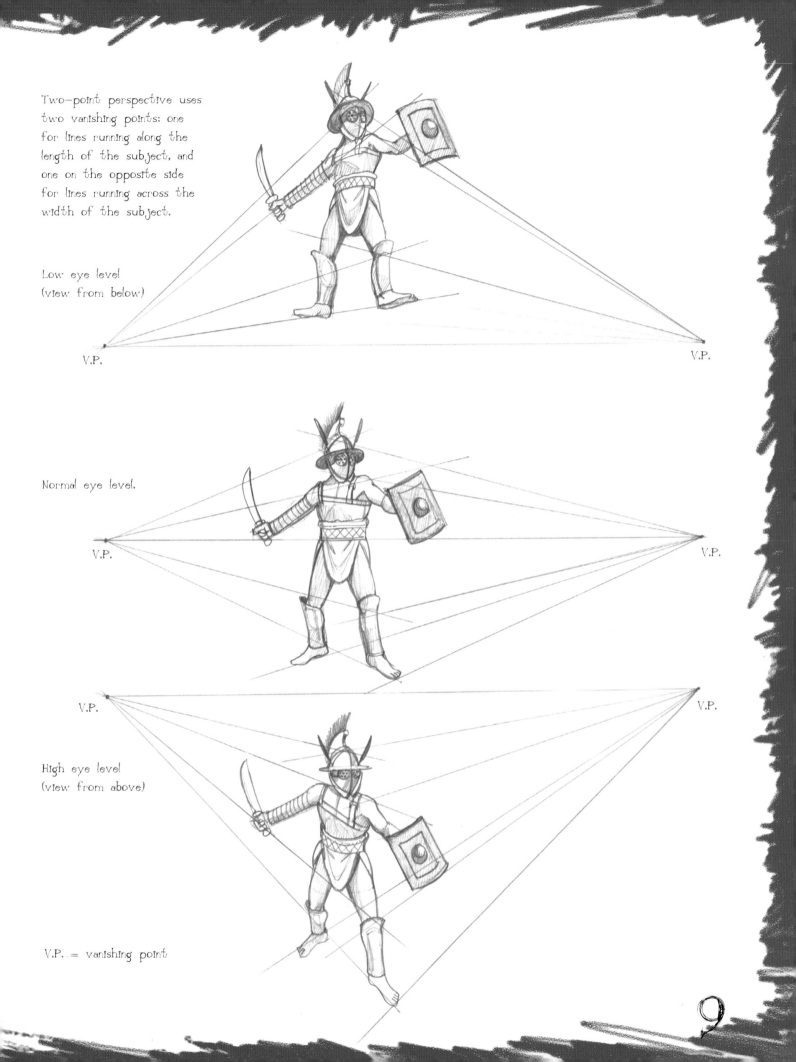

Two-point perspective uses two vanishing points: one for lines running along the length of the subject, and one on the opposite side for lines running across the width of the subject.

Low eye level (view from below)

V.P.

V.P.

Normal eye level.

V.P.

V.P.

V.P.

V.P.

High eye level (view from above)

V.P. = vanishing point

9

# Using Photos

**D**rawing from photographs of real fighting figures can help you develop your drawing skills and also your eye for detail.

Make a tracing of a photograph and draw a grid of squares over it.

Now draw another grid on your drawing paper, enlarging or reducing the squares but keeping the same proportions as your tracing grid. You can now copy the shapes from each square of your tracing to your drawing paper, using the grid as a guide.

To make your drawing look three-dimensional, decide which side the light is coming from, and put in areas of shadow on the opposite side.

Sketch in an overall tone to create interest and a sense of movement. Pay attention to the position of the figures on the paper. This is called composition.

# Action Poses

**P**ractice basic poses and quick stick figure drawings to get a sense of action into your basic poses. Getting the movement right in these early stages will make your completed drawing look better.

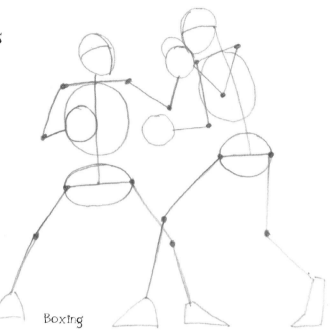

Boxing

Judo

Sword fight

Wrestling

Blocking a kick

High kick

Using construction lines from
the start of your drawing
helps you create figures
with a more solid, 3-D feel.

Kendo

13

# Ninja Assassin

**T**hese stealthy warriors would attack under the cloak of darkness and were used by noblemen to assassinate their opponents.

Draw a curved line for the sword.

Add ovals for hands.

Sketch in the arms with dots for joints.

Add basic shapes for the feet.

Draw ovals for the head, body, and hips. Add lines for the spine and hips.

Draw lines for the legs, with dots for joints.

## Composition

By framing your drawing with a square or a rectangle, you can make it look completely different.

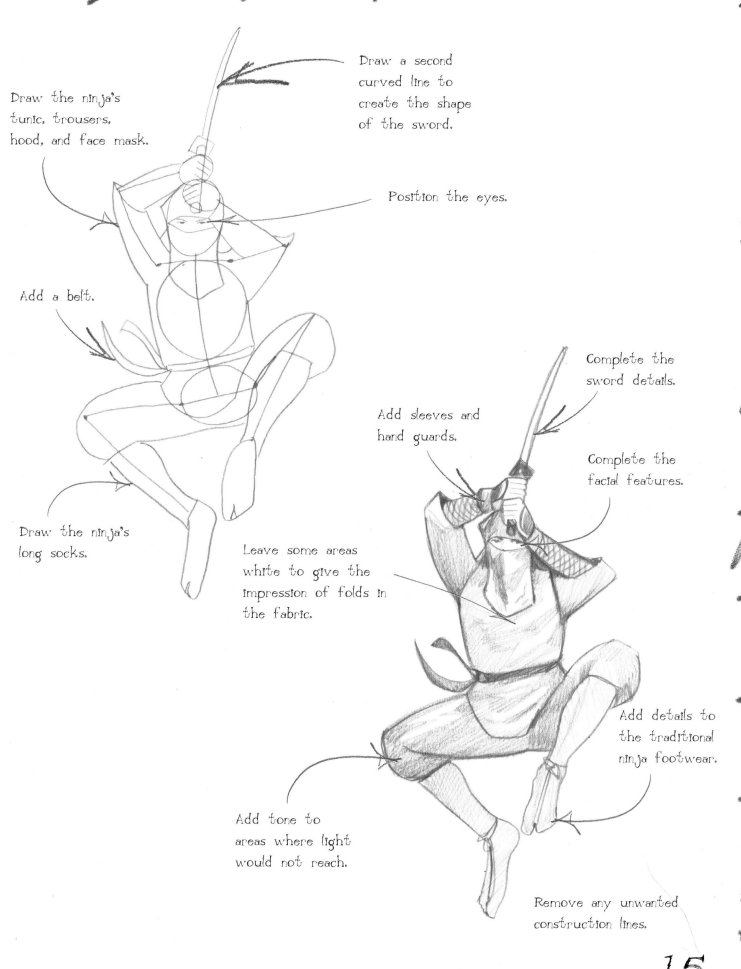

Draw the ninja's tunic, trousers, hood, and face mask.

Draw a second curved line to create the shape of the sword.

Position the eyes.

Add a belt.

Draw the ninja's long socks.

Complete the sword details.

Add sleeves and hand guards.

Complete the facial features.

Leave some areas white to give the impression of folds in the fabric.

Add details to the traditional ninja footwear.

Add tone to areas where light would not reach.

Remove any unwanted construction lines.

15

# Karate

**K**arate is the martial art of the empty hand. In competition, each opponent uses only his hands and feet to punch or kick until his rival is overcome.

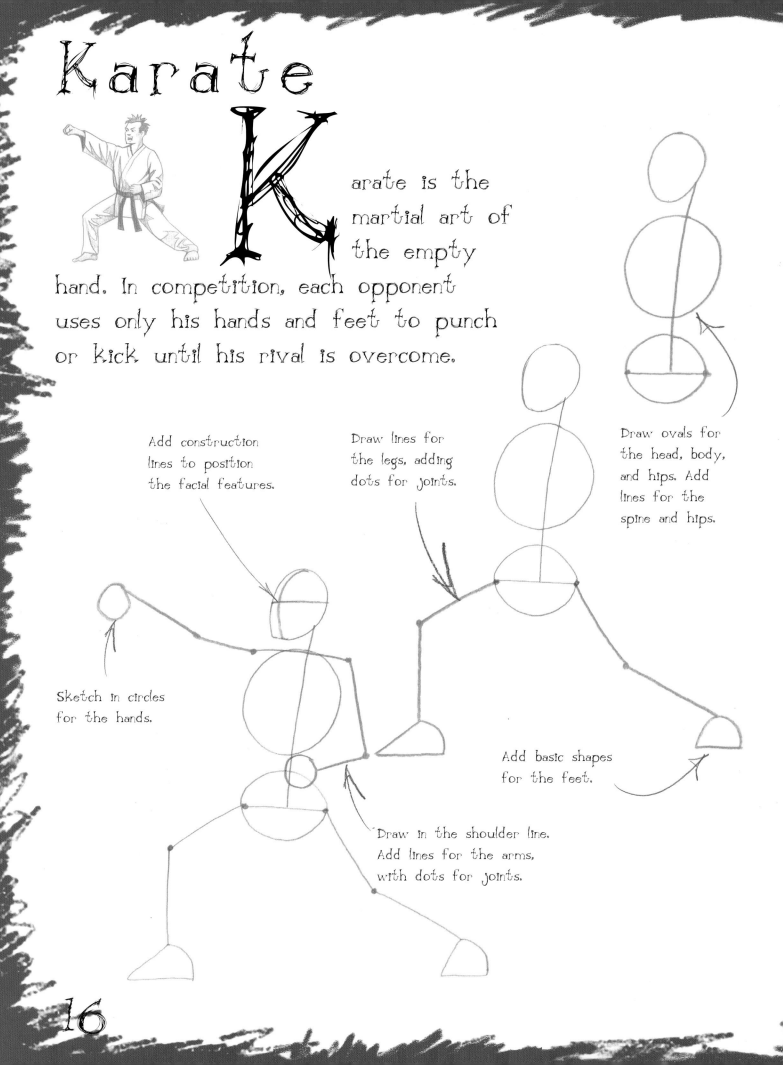

Draw ovals for the head, body, and hips. Add lines for the spine and hips.

Add construction lines to position the facial features.

Draw lines for the legs, adding dots for joints.

Sketch in circles for the hands.

Add basic shapes for the feet.

Draw in the shoulder line. Add lines for the arms, with dots for joints.

Add spiky hair.

Sketch in the expressive facial features using the construction lines as a guide.

Draw the shape of the clenched fist inside the circle.

Add the tunic of the *karategi* (the karate uniform).

Draw in a belt.

Add the karategi trousers.

Add more detail to the shape of the feet.

Finish drawing the fist.

Complete the facial details.

Add tone to areas where light wouldn't reach.

Add lines and tone to show the folds in the karategi.

Add tone to the belt.

Finish off the feet.

Remove any unwanted construction lines.

# Karate Kick

I n karate the body is used as a weapon. This karate expert is using the ball of her foot for a front flying kick.

Draw ovals for the head, body, and hips. Add lines for the spine and hips.

Add construction lines to position the facial features.

Sketch in oval shapes for the hands.

Draw the shoulder line. Add arms, with dots for joints.

Sketch in basic shapes for the feet.

Draw lines for the legs, with dots for joints.

## Using a Mirror
Try looking at your drawing in a mirror. Seeing it in reverse can help you spot mistakes.

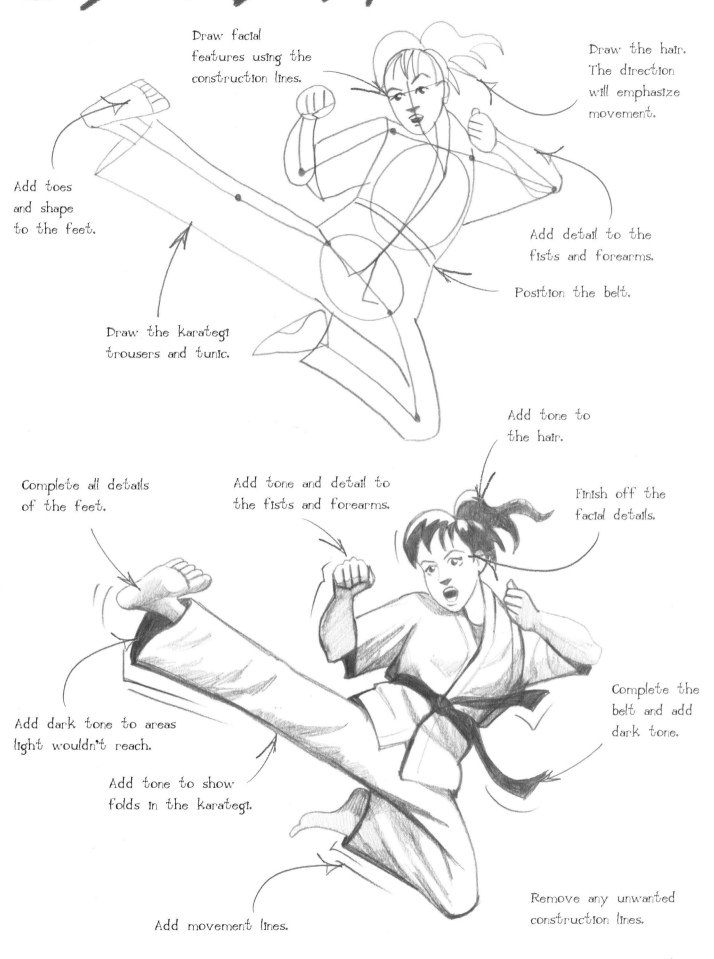

Draw facial features using the construction lines.

Draw the hair. The direction will emphasize movement.

Add toes and shape to the feet.

Add detail to the fists and forearms.

Position the belt.

Draw the karategi trousers and tunic.

Add tone to the hair.

Complete all details of the feet.

Add tone and detail to the fists and forearms.

Finish off the facial details.

Add dark tone to areas light wouldn't reach.

Complete the belt and add dark tone.

Add tone to show folds in the karategi.

Remove any unwanted construction lines.

Add movement lines.

19

# Samurai Battle

Samurai warriors fought in accordance with Japanese rules of honor and pride. They used a range of weapons, which included incredibly sharp swords called *katanas*.

Draw ovals for the heads, bodies, and hips. Add lines for the spines and hips.

This samurai is seen in profile so the line of the spine is on the left side.

Sketch in ovals for the hands.

Add lines for the arms, with dots for the joints.

Add lines for the blade of each sword.

Add lines for the legs, with dots for the joints.

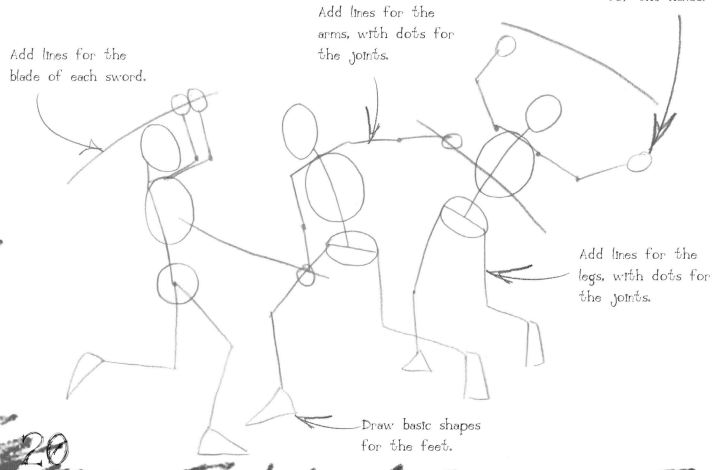

Draw basic shapes for the feet.

Add hair to each samurai.

Draw the facial features.

Sketch in more shape to each sword.

Each samurai's robe is tied in the middle.

Using the construction lines as a guide, add the samurai's traditional clothing.

Add tone to areas where light wouldn't reach.

Finish off the facial details.

Add tone to the hair.

Add lines and tone to show folds in the fabric. Leave some areas white.

Complete the detail of the clothing by adding a pattern.

Finish the details of the feet.

Complete the details of each costume.

Remove any unwanted construction lines.

21

# Armored Samurai

These two heavily armored samurai are from the Genpei War. The striking katana (samurai sword) is being blocked by the *naginata* (the staff).

Draw ovals for the heads, bodies, and hips. Add lines for the spines and hips.

Add lines for the arms, with dots for the joints.

Add a long line with a curved end for the naginata.

Draw basic shapes for the helmets.

Add basic hand shapes.

Draw basic shapes for the feet.

Draw lines for the legs, with dots for the joints.

Complete the shape of the naginata.

Draw fingers on each hand.

Draw the sleeves and wide samurai pants.

Draw the facial features.

Add the complex decoration of the helmets.

Add the large plates of armour.

Sketch in the legs, indicating armor.

Add tone to areas light wouldn't reach.

Finish the facial features.

Complete the samurai helmets and costume detail.

Add zigzag details to the armor to show how it is made.

Add tone to show the shape and movement of the pants.

Complete the details of the naginata and katana.

Add armor to the legs and complete the feet.

Remove any unwanted construction lines.

23

# Kendo

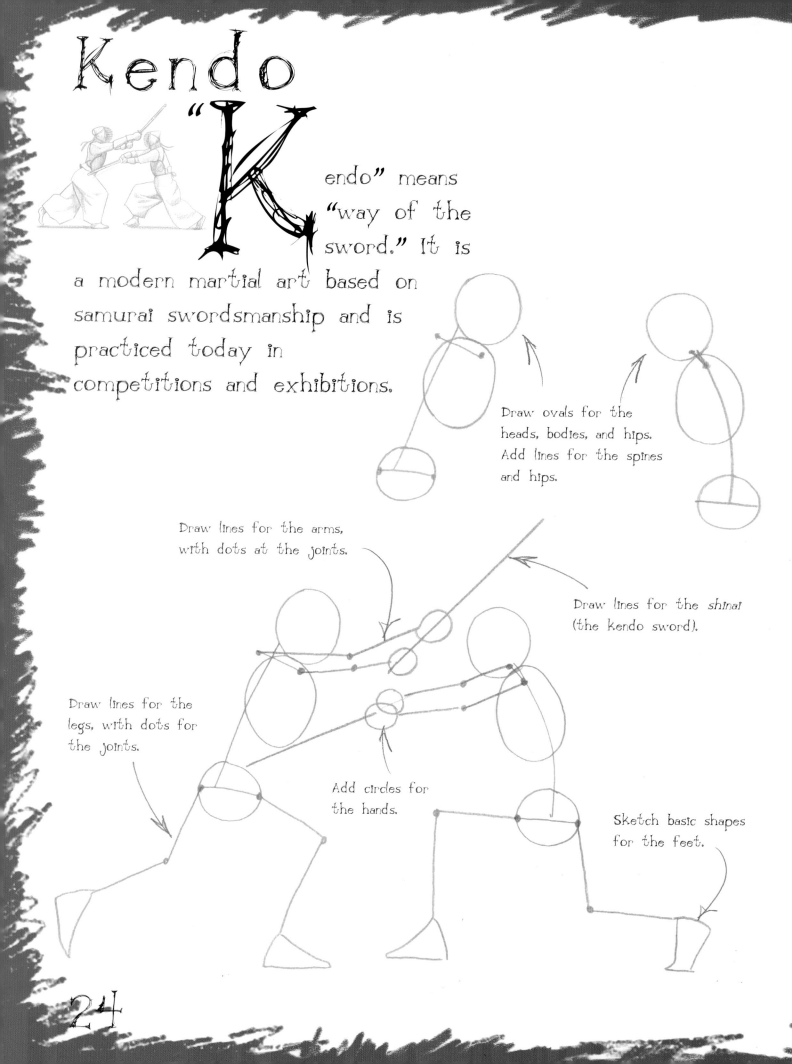

"**K**endo" means "way of the sword." It is a modern martial art based on samurai swordsmanship and is practiced today in competitions and exhibitions.

Draw ovals for the heads, bodies, and hips. Add lines for the spines and hips.

Draw lines for the arms, with dots at the joints.

Draw lines for the *shinai* (the kendo sword).

Draw lines for the legs, with dots for the joints.

Add circles for the hands.

Sketch basic shapes for the feet.

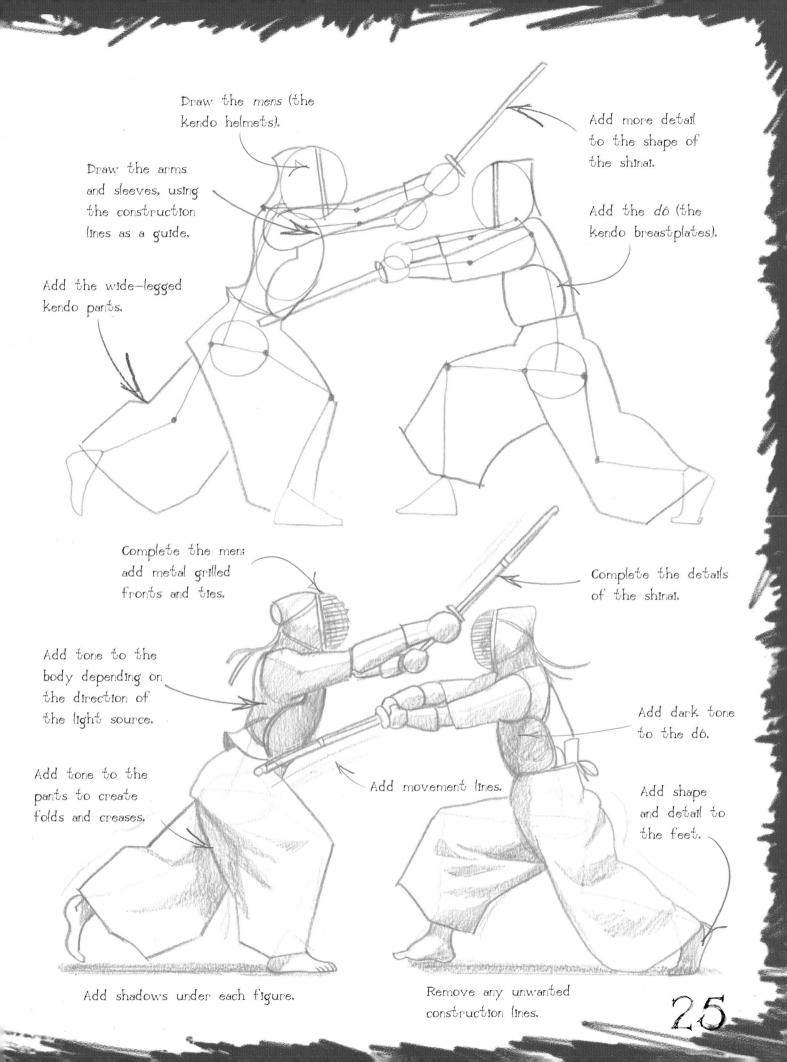

Draw the *mens* (the kendo helmets).

Draw the arms and sleeves, using the construction lines as a guide.

Add the wide-legged kendo pants.

Add more detail to the shape of the shinai.

Add the *dô* (the kendo breastplates).

Complete the men; add metal grilled fronts and ties.

Complete the details of the shinai.

Add tone to the body depending on the direction of the light source.

Add dark tone to the dô.

Add tone to the pants to create folds and creases.

Add movement lines.

Add shape and detail to the feet.

Add shadows under each figure.

Remove any unwanted construction lines.

25

# Greek Warriors

These two Bronze Age Greek hoplite warriors are from warring states. They are fighting shield to shield. Cities like Athens and Sparta were deadly enemies, fighting for supremacy over land and trade routes.

Draw ovals for the heads, bodies, and hips. Add lines for the spines and hips.

Draw two large ovals for shields.

Draw a line for each sword.

Draw lines for the arms, with dots for the joints.

Add circles for the hands.

Sketch in lines for the legs, with dots for the joints.

Sketch in basic shapes for the feet.

Draw the distinctive helmet shapes.

Add more detail to the swords.

Draw the shape of the arms, using the construction lines as a guide.

Add the curved decoration to each helmet.

Sketch in the body armor and tunics.

Add shape to the legs, using the construction lines as a guide.

Draw the leg armor.

Add designs and battle scars to each shield.

Complete all details to each helmet.

Add tone to the arms.

Add hair.

Complete all details of the armor.

Add both scabbards.

Add tone to the leg armor.

Add toes and all details of the feet.

Add tone to areas light wouldn't reach.

Remove any unwanted construction lines.

27

# Judo

# J

Judo is a modern martial art. Its name means the "gentle way." The object of a competition is to throw an opponent to the ground, immobilizing him, and to force his submission using specific maneuvers.

Draw ovals for the heads, bodies, and hips. Add lines for the spines and hips.

Draw lines for the arms, with dots for the joints. The arms overlap as the figures grab hold of each other.

Add basic shapes for hands.

Sketch in construction lines to position the facial features.

Add lines for the legs, with dots for the joints.

Draw basic shapes for the feet.

Using the construction lines as a guide, add the tunic of the *judogi* (the judo uniform).

Draw the hairline.

Add the belts.

Sketch in the basic details of each face.

Use the construction line to draw the *judogi* pants.

Pay careful attention to which leg is in front of which.

Add detail to the hands.

Finish off the hair and facial features.

Add dark tone to the belts.

Add tone to areas where light wouldn't reach.

Add toes and complete the feet.

Add lines and tone to show folds and movement in the fabric.

Remove any unwanted construction lines.

# Roman Gladiators

The gladiatorial games were loved by all in ancient Rome. Here a retiarius (with net and trident) battles a murmillo, the gladiator with the sword and shield.

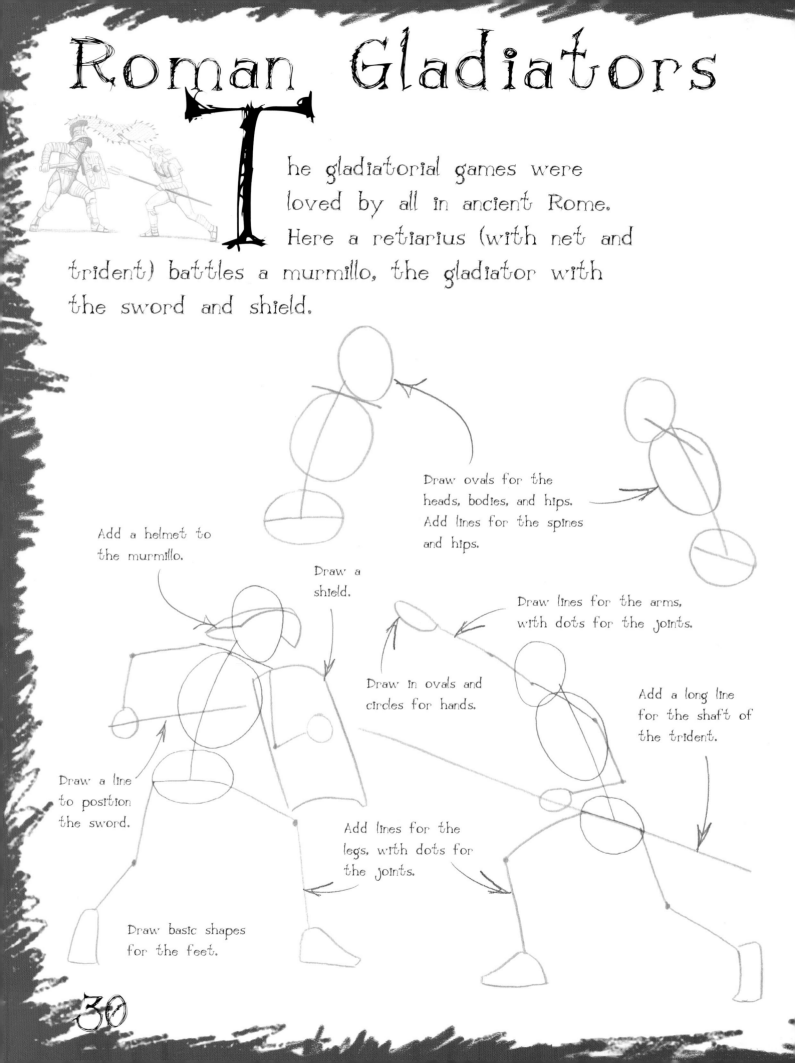

Draw ovals for the heads, bodies, and hips. Add lines for the spines and hips.

Add a helmet to the murmillo.

Draw a shield.

Draw lines for the arms, with dots for the joints.

Draw in ovals and circles for hands.

Add a long line for the shaft of the trident.

Draw a line to position the sword.

Add lines for the legs, with dots for the joints.

Draw basic shapes for the feet.

Sketch in the shape of the murmillo's helmet and sword.

Sketch in the flowing shape to show the net being thrown.

Add fingers and detail to the hands.

Sketch in all head details.

Indicate shoulder, arm, and leg armor.

Draw the shape of the arms using the construction lines.

Draw the trident.

Sketch in the armored sections of the legs.

Add the arm, the body armor, and a belt.

Add all details to finish the net.

Complete the details of the helmet and all body armor.

Complete the details of the head.

Complete the shield decoration.

Draw the details of the armor.

Complete the trident.

Add tone to areas light wouldn't reach.

Add all details to the feet.

Remove any unwanted construction lines.

# Glossary

**composition** (kom–puh–ZIH–shun) The arrangement of the parts of a picture on the drawing paper.

**construction lines** (kun–STRUK–shun LYNZ) Guidelines used in the early stages of a drawing. They are usually erased later.

**light source** (LYT SORS) The direction from which the light seems to come in a drawing.

**perspective** (per–SPEK–tiv) A method of drawing in which near objects are shown larger than faraway objects to give an impression of depth.

**pose** (POHZ) The position assumed by a figure.

**proportion** (pruh–POR–shun) The correct relationship of scale between each part of the drawing.

**silhouette** (sih–luh–WET) A drawing that shows only a flat dark shape, like a shadow.

**vanishing point** (VA–nih–shing POYNT) The place in a perspective drawing where parallel lines appear to meet.

# Index

# Web Sites

Due to the changing nature of Internet links, PowerKids Press has developed an online list of Web sites related to the subject of this book. This site is updated regularly. Please use this link to access the list: